THE LANCASTER CANAL IN FOCUS

Janet Rigby

Landy Publishing 2007

ISBN 978 1 872895 72 7

A catalogue record of this book is available from the British Library.

Printed by Nayler Group Ltd. Accrington.
Tel: 01254 234247

Landy Publishing have also published:

Life on the Lancaster Canal by Janet Rigby
Lancashire's Medieval Monasteries by Brian Marshall
Northward by Anthony Hewitson **
Bolland Forest & The Hodder Valley by Greenwood & Bolton **
A History of Pilling by F Sobee **
Glimpses of Glasson Dock by Ruth Z Roskell
Preston in Focus by Stephen Sartin
A Preston Mixture edited by Bob Dobson **
Play Up, Higher Walton by Peter Holme
Edgworth to Crowthorne: History of a Lancashire Orphanage by Anita Forth

Those marked** are available at a reduced price when ordered direct from the publisher.

A full list is available from: Landy Publishing
'Acorns', 3 Staining Rise, Staining, Blackpool, FY3 0BU
Tel/Fax 01253 895678 (24 hrs) e-mail: peggie@peggiedobson.wanadoo.co.uk

INTRODUCTION

During my research on my first book *'Life on the Lancaster Canal'* I came across photographs and postcards of the canal, not only of scenery, but pictures portraying the working life of the Lancaster boatman. It was not an easy task. If I had chosen a busier waterway such as the Leeds-Liverpool, it would have been far easier, as they are much more numerous. My publisher suggested I do a pictorial book that would enable me to include those images missed out of the first one because of lack of space. I also wanted to find images that had not been published before and was extremely lucky in that a recent introduction to Joe Robinson (the little lad on the front cover) provided me with access to an album of wonderful photographs. Joe's family, were, along with the Ashcrofts, one of the main families on the canal and his father, Joe senior, had set out with his camera to skilfully record their working life in the nineteen twenties on the Wigan Coal & Iron Company's boats *'Express'* and *'Kendal'*. I feel very privileged to be the means by which these pictures can be enjoyed by others.

Whilst postcards are a wonderful source, it is not always easy to locate the exact position the photograph was taken and in which direction we are looking but I have tried where possible to identify the bridge numbers. There are many people who have helped me compile this, the first pictorial book on the Lancaster Canal. Without them this book would not have been possible. I wish to thank the following for loan of photographs, John Gavan; the late May Sharp (nee Ashcroft;, Cyril Thompson, (grandson of Lawrence Baines); Jim Heron, the late Edward Paget-Tomlinson (for his drawings); Michael Hargreaves; Darren Benson; Ruth Roskell; Hilda Thompson; Mark Shuttleworth; John Parkinson; Dorothy Green, (granddaughter of James Baines); Colin Barnes; Bill Robinson; Trevor Hughes; Percy Duff; Albert Clayton; Eric Bell; the Lancaster Canal Trust, the Canal Card Collector's Society; Ellesmere Port Boat Museum and the Lancaster Maritime Museum. I also wish to thank those not listed here who have helped in any way with snippets of information and also a special thank you to my husband David, a descendant of the Ashcroft family, for his patience and help with local knowledge of the Ashton area.

Janet Rigby, St Annes on Sea – April 2007

Packet boats began in 1798 between Preston and Lancaster, and then ran to Kendal when the canal extended throughout by 1819. In 1833 *'Swallow'* and *'Swiftsure'* followed the first of the swift boats, *'Water Witch'*. A fourth one *'Crewdson'* named after the chairman of the Canal Company was provided to connect with the North Union train at Preston. On the same day the railway opened to Kendal, (21 September 1846) the passenger packets ceased. After being taken out of service, the two remaining boats *'Crewdson'* and the *'Swiftsure'* were stored in the Packet Boat House at Aldcliffe until the end of the 19th century. *'Swiftsure'* was later dismantled but the *'Crewdson'*, re-named *'Waterwitch II,'* was used as an inspection boat, with its cabin shortened, for many years. It was eventually broken up in 1929, but a replica can be seen at the Lancaster Maritime Museum. This photograph was taken about 1900.

LANCASTER CANAL.

THE swift sailing PACKET BOATS between Lancaster and Kendal, SAIL daily as follows:—

From Lancaster ... 7 30 a.m.   12 0
From Kendal ... 8 30 do.   1 30 p.m.

The Boats from Lancaster will be despatched on arrival of the respective Trains from the South, and the Boats from Kendal will be in time for the Trains to the South at 1 10 p.m., and 5 30 p.m.

Fares between Lancaster and Kendal, First Cabin, 3s.; Second Cabin, 2s.

Breakfast and Refreshments provided on Board. The Boats are warmed in cold weather.

An Omnibus between the Railway and Packet Stations at Lancaster, free of charge.   Aug. 24, 1842.

This building (right) on Canal Head North, Kendal was thought to have been the original Packet Boat Office, The sign shows it here as the offices of Wigan Coal & Iron Company.

At the southern end in Preston is the *'Lamb and Packet'* pub, at the corner of Friargate and Kendal Street, formerly Canal Street. The pub is named after this type of packet boat, and the lamb is on Preston's coat of arms.

This photograph of *'Waterwitch II'* was taken between 1880-1890, before the cabin was shortened. After being taken out of storage in 1915 it was offered to Lancaster Corporation who rented a piece of land on the canal bank near Aldcliffe Road from Mr J M Pickard, for an annual rent of one shilling. Here it lay for the next fourteen years on display, before it was broken up.

The packet boathouse at Aldcliffe (near Bridge 97) was used for repairing packet boats between 1833 and 1843. The boathouse is skew to the canal to allow the boats to enter and leave. It had a hoist to lift the boats to the upper floors.

'Waterwitch II' on the canal bank near Aldcliffe about 1915.

5

Loading *'Richard No. 31'* with coal at the Marsh Lane end of Preston basin - coal and limestone represented eighty per cent of traffic until 1906, when Holme Park Quarry closed, leaving coal and *'slack'* (coal dust) as the main cargo.

The round trip to Kendal took a week, twice as long as to Lancaster. Non-bulk cargoes were gunpowder to Wakefield's Factory at Sedgwick, and machinery and textile parts from Lancaster. This lasted until 1947 when the canal-side mills turned to oil.

An advert from Seed's Directory, 1904

Coal is being tipped from the railway wagon on to *'Kendal'* by use of a tippler at Preston.

Joseph Robinson and his *'helpers'* starting the heavy task of discharging about fifty tons of coal from the boat, which would probably take all day.

Agnes Robinson at the tiller of *'Kendal'* No. 33 as the coal is being tipped into the boat from the railway wagons.

A cargo of grass, cut by the boatmen from the canal bank on the way, to be used for fodder for the horses. The bucket is filled with fresh honeysuckle.

'Kendal' setting off from the wharf

The southern end of the Preston Basin in 1938. Just beyond the railway wagons crossing the end of the canal, the tram road continued southwards to Walton Summit, first passing under the buildings on Fishergate seen on the horizon. To the extreme left of the picture is the tower of the Baptist Church, one of the few buildings remaining today on Fishergate. Next to it are Loxham's Garages.

These two pictures of Preston wharf were taken in 1897; the one on the left is of the eastern arm. The entrances can be seen to the goods warehouses and the picture on the right shows two lifting bridges and the shunting of the wagons being undertaken by horse traction. The buildings on the right are in Ladywell Street, which ran down to the canal basin.

Aqueduct Bridge which carried the canal over Aqueduct Street, Preston, photographed in 1964, shortly before demolition. In 1887 a plot to blow up the bridge with dynamite was foiled. If successful it would have resulted in the town being flooded. The attempt was blamed on the *'Fenians'* or Irishmen who were opposed to the English presence in Ireland.

Inquest.—On the 20th inst. an inquest was held before Rd. Newsham, Esq. Mayor, at the Town Hall, Preston, on the body of R. W. Hornby, of Kirkham, tailor, who was killed on Wednesday night, by falling over the battlements of the Aqueduct Bridge, across the old Lancaster lane, near the Marsh End, Preston. Wm. Anderton, tallow-chandler, stated, that the deceased was about 83 years of age; that on Wednesday night about eleven o'clock he was with the deceased, when they stopped at the bridge which carries the canal across the old Lancaster lane, where the deceased, in attempting to rest himself, slipped over the battlement, and fell upon a bank, or cop, below the bridge. Medical assistance was immediately procured, but it was of no avail. —Verdict, *Accidental Death.*

The canal along Fylde Road going northwards with Bretherton's Corn Mill in the distance. None of the buildings are there today and the whole area has been built over.

Cutting from Lancaster Gazette 1836 reporting a tragic accident on the bridge.

The *Lime Kiln'* Public House stands near to the site of the old lime kiln in Aqueduct Street, where the limestone rock would be transhipped to the kiln where it was burned to a fine powder before being spread over the fields or combined with sand to form mortar for building works. Limestone rock had been transported from the Kendal area in the barges which had carried coal Northwards.

Right is a disused lime kiln at the bottom of Fylde Road and Water Lane, Preston.

The curved entrance to the former *'Boatman's Arms'* in Marsh Lane, Preston, where the boatmen stabled their horses. One of the last reminders of the canal in Preston, it was demolished in 2007 to make way for student accommodation. It was built around 1900.

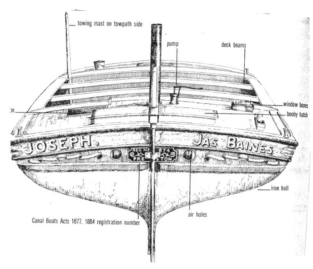

Canal Boats Acts 1877, 1884 registration number

Lancaster boats were 14 ft. 6 inches wide and 72 foot long with a maximum capacity of 52 tons, and were always horse drawn, sometimes by two horses. The Canal Boats Acts of 1877 and 1884 required all working boats to register with the local authority and were given a numbered certificate, the number painted on the side of the boat. The earlier boats were made of wood but lack of repair facilities on the canal meant they were constructed of iron after about 1890, mostly by W Allsupp of Preston. They were not as highly decorative as their Midland counterparts. The cabin space was about fourteen feet wide and sixteen foot in length. The bed space was divided up by use of bed boards according to the size of the boatman's family.   (Drawings by Edward Paget-Tomlinson).

A postcard sent to boatman James Churchhouse in 1916 by James Baines asking for help in unloading at Lancaster. Such was the speed and reliability of the postal service, sending a message ahead in this fashion must have been commonplace. The 'Iron Duke' was named in honour of the Duke of Wellington, an English hero still honoured as a soldier and statesman.

'Herbert No. 34', in the ownership of S Kent. Its registration was surrendered in 1948 under the name of 'Ashcroft Carriers Ltd' along with 'Kenneth' 'Herbert' 'Wasp' 'Benjamin' and 'Ann'. The boats were sold to the Ashcroft family in 1944, when the Baines' ceased trading. By this time trade was declining and was only to last another three years.

'Herbert' ended its days as a landing stage at Peel on the Isle of Man.

The Baines family had always been boatmen but it is not certain when they formed Baines Brothers. In a 1922 Barrett's Trade Directory they were listed as 'boat owners'. Their association with the canal went back to the early 1800s when a John Baines was captain of one of the packet boats.

.

'Sarah No. 28' under repair. From the wharf at Preston there were two small branches which had a yard where boats were pulled onto a slipway for repair or maintenance.

Thomas Ashcroft on 'Ann No. 15' at the tiller.

A team of canal company workmen take a break from maintenance work and pose for a cameraman in the 1940s next to the maintenance boat 'Stella'. This boat, formerly owned by S R Thompson, was dismantled in 1915.

'*Express* No. 7' laden with coal heading North at Salwick wharf, which once served the nearby market town of Kirkham. Salwick is now a favourite mooring spot for cruisers. '*Station Cottages*', owned by the Duchy of Lancaster are on the left. They are still there today and typify the simple style of the original canal-side domestic architecture.

This undated postcard of '*Beehive No. 37*' at Myerscough with the '*Roebuck*' public house on the far right. The small building by the second boat is now a water point for pleasure boaters. In 1881 ''*Beehive*' was crewed by the Darlington family.

A boat laden with coal near Garstang, around 1934. The horse is just out of sight of the photograph, as you can see the tow rope fastened to the white topped poles.

A postcard dated about 1909 at Bonds, heading North towards Garstang. 'Stella' was owned at the time by the firm of S R Thompson of Lancaster, and so Stella was perhaps a member of that family.

Front view of a horse as it pulls a boat through a bridge.

This is a bank rangers' boat at the Wyre Aqueduct, Garstang. The rangers were responsible for a length of about seven miles of canal and their boat was often referred to as a *'muck boat'*, an oblong boat with a flat front. They usually worked in teams and would go along the canal carrying out repairs, mending breaches, looking for leaks and mowing grass. Two of the canal company's boats were the *'Olive'* and the *'Stella'*.

'Pet' about 1895 at the old Penny Street Bridge, Lancaster, which was replaced a few years later. After delivering her last cargo to the mills in 1946, she was used as a maintenance boat before being converted into a trip boat and re-named *'Lady Fiona'*. In 2003 she was taken out of service for restoration to her former working state but the future of the boat (2007) is now uncertain.

'Benjamin No. 48' unloading at Storey's Mill, Lancaster. This mill was unusual in that it had a large tub on an overhead gantry and employed two coal heavers to discharge the vessel's cargo into this, but at all other wharves, cargoes were off-loaded by barrow and shovel.

'Kenneth' at Bolton-le-Sands.

Horses were always used to tow the boats on this canal but about 1918 two *'steamboats'* the *'Asland'* and the *'Cricket'* were brought off the Leeds- Liverpool Canal for a trial period by Thompson & Co. of Lancaster.

This postcard, posted 1920, shows a steamer towing four boats at Bolton le Sands with *'Sarah'*, owned by W I Turner & Co. at the rear. It was not a success; there were problems getting up the locks without horses and it was not long before they reverted to horses which were used until business on the canal ceased in 1947.

Postcard of Bridge 128 at Carnforth about 1905 - the boat heading South is thought to be the *'James'*. Steering it is Thomas Robinson who lived in the house on the right of the picture which is in Kellet Lane. Even though they had a house, Thomas's son Joseph attended different schools along the canal and above right is his attendance record from 1904 – 1908 at a Preston school. The young boy is James Robinson. A development of houses has recently (2006) been built on the right bank at the far side of the bridge.

Dan Ashcroft and *'Iron Duke No. 9'* at Holme Park at the spot where his daughter, four year old Nellie drowned on 7 September 1907. He was loading the boat with broken limestone and whilst he went to move the boat, Nellie fell in and drowned. There were many reported cases of drownings in the canal and many canal people never learned to swim. *'Iron Duke'* is mentioned on page 9.

'*May No 35*' approaching Tewitfield Locks about 1910. Apart from those on the Glasson branch, these eight locks were the only ones on the canal. They were finally closed in 1968 after years of disuse to make way for the M6 motorway. This now marks the end of navigation on the '*Lanky*' but the locks can still be reached on foot. Hopes are high that the '*Northern Reaches*' will be restored to enable craft to sail up to Kendal. A new marina is being constructed at the Tewitfield terminus in anticipation of this.

John Shuttleworth (right) was the last lock-keeper and lived at '*Top Lock Cottage*' (above) (now demolished), until the locks closed.

'*Express No 7'* entering Tewitfield Locks in the 1920s. Note the distinctive decoration of a typical Wigan Coal & Iron Company boat, which had rows of white, five-pointed stars along the gunwale and across the stern.

Drawing of horse entering Hincaster tunnel by Edward Paget-Tomlinson.

'*Ann No 15'* entering Hincaster Tunnel, with Tom Ashcroft on the tiller. It is the only tunnel on the canal, built to take barges to the Gunpowder Works at Sedgwick. The horses were taken over the tunnel along the horse path and the barges were hauled through by means of a rope fixed to a side wall or were '*legged*' through by the boatmen pushing against the sides with their feet. The canal bed is now dry and the vegetation overgrown but in 1980 the tunnel portals were restored by the Royal Engineers. This work was arranged by the Lancaster Canal Trust.

The Kendal canal basin pictured here about 1897 was opened in 1819 and consisted of four wharves, on each of the north and south sides, two wharves at its east end and a pair of warehouses along the west end. In 1824 the canal company sold some of the land for Kendal Gas Works, thus creating a coal traffic which lasted for 120 years. Whilst it is unlikely that there will be another working wharf at the Northern end of the canal, if things go to plan there will be a basin, marina and landing stage. The heavily laden boat at the back of *'Kendal'* is the *'James'*.

Joseph Robinson is seen here discharging coal at the gas works In the 1920s. His father, Thomas had also worked on the canal but around 1930 Joseph decided to leave and went to work at Cottam Brickworks.

John Tickle (1905-1988) who worked the canal with his foster parents, Joshua Robinson and his wife Jane (nee Hampton). Joshua was the brother of Thomas Robinson who also appears in this book, and was formerly a coal dealer. This is a photograph from about 1920.

Below is a set of *'horse stairs'* near the canal. The narrower set to the right was for the *'horse lad'*.

'Dinah' the much loved horse of the Robinson family.

'Dinah' towing a fully laden *'Express'* and being taken over a canal bridge by Agnes Robinson.

A boat at Ashton going North just past Cottam Mill Bridge No. 16. Beetham's Farm is on the left.

A canal horse decked up in its finery. perhaps for the Preston Guild Procession of 1902 or 1922. The location is not known but is thought to be in a Preston street. The photograph is interesting for the dress of the lady and the boatman, who is in his working clothes.

Mary Jane Ashcroft at Bell Fold (Bridge No. 35) at Woodplumpton.

An early picture of the Ashcrofts at Hest Bank.

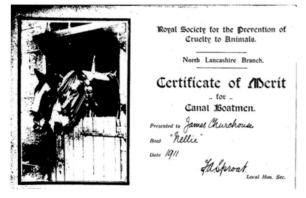

The Lancaster boatmen were renowned for their kind treatment to their horses, as these certificates awarded to James Churchhouse show. He also received certificates for the horses working on 'May', *Olive*'. and *'Stella.'* The Humane Officer would inspect the boatmen's horses regularly.

Thomas Ashcroft, was an accomplished horseman. The canal horses were usually bought from traders at Lancaster.

The goods warehouses at the eastern leg of Preston basin - after trade ceased in 1947, it fell into disrepair and was eventually drained and filled in. The site is now occupied by an Aldi Superstore. Arkright's Furniture warehouse in the centre was located in Corporation Street and is listed in the street index of the 1909 Ordnance Map of Preston.

This scene is looking towards Fishergate, Preston and the railway line alongside the canal ran under Marsh Lane, where coal and slack was loaded into the boats from the railway wagons, which had been delivered by train from Wigan.

These pictures were taken about 1960, by a British Rail photographer a couple of years before the whole area was demolished, filled in and built over. The canal quickly became an area of squalor and neglect, with unwanted items dumped in the water as can be seen below. This scene is practically the same location as that on page 8, showing the lifting bridges.

The above picture is looking towards Marsh Lane
and the building on the wharf may have been a coal office.

'Kenneth' at Ben Baker's yard at Catforth, in 1955, just before being broken up. All of the Lancaster working boats suffered this fate with the exception of 'Pet' which later became a trip boat, the 'Lady Fiona'.

Some of the buildings were abandoned and left to decay, including the boathouse at Aldcliffe adjacent to Bridge 97 at Lancaster. When the remaining packet boats were taken out of service they were put into storage here. The boathouse has now been restored.

THE CANAL, HEST BANK.

'Benjamin' is seen here in use as a 'floating office' in front of the small trip boat, looking North towards Bridge No. 118, from which point the canal comes nearest the sea, only a few hundred yards away at high water. Its registration, along with those of 'Kenneth' 'Herbert' 'Wasp' and 'Ann' had been surrendered in 1948 under the name of 'Ashcroft Carriers Ltd.' It was not used for very long and the boat was sunk in the basin by the Lune Aqueduct, later brought to the surface and broken up.

An unusual case of 'horse rustling' on the Lancaster Canal.

THURSDAY.

Criminal business was resumed before Mr. Justice Collins on Thursday morning at 10 30. His Lordship was accompanied on the Bench by the High Sheriff, Under Sheriff, and Mr. Davis (Clerk.)

THEFT OF A CANAL TOWING HORSE.

Thomas Knowles, 17, hawker (a native of Lancaster), pleaded not guilty to an indictment for stealing a horse, value £1, the property of James Vickers, at Preston, on June 5th.—Mr. McKeand prosecuted, and said the horse belonged to James Vickers, of the canal boat "Bell," which travels between Preston and Kendal. The horse was put into a field at Ashton, near Preston, but was missed next day, when prisoner sold it to the Blackpool Tower Company for food for the lions for the sum of 25s. The police interfered

An unusual case of 'horse rustling' occurred when Thomas Knowles of Lancaster was accused of stealing a horse belonging to James Vickers, boatman of 'Bell' and selling it to Blackpool Zoo for twenty five shillings, 'for feed for the lions'. He was sentenced to six months hard labour because of previous convictions, 'and the horse's life was spared from its designed fate.'

(Extract from 'Lancaster Guardian' October 1896).

"Didn't we have a lovely time the day we went to Catforth" - what would today's Health and Safety inspectors make of this boatload out one Sunday near Beetham's Farm, Cottam, with Cottam Mill Bridge (No. 16) in the distance.

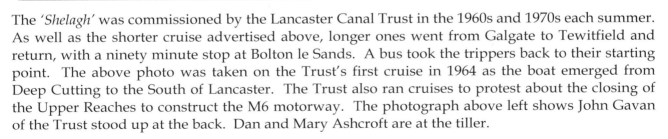

ASSOCIATION FOR RESTORATION OF
THE LANCASTER CANAL

— A —

Cruise on the Lancaster Canal

ON SUNDAY, 8th MAY, 1966.

Departure : 10 a.m. at GARSTANG BASIN
(Price includes Free Bus back to Garstang from Lancaster)

PRICE : 9/–

The *'Shelagh'* was commissioned by the Lancaster Canal Trust in the 1960s and 1970s each summer. As well as the shorter cruise advertised above, longer ones went from Galgate to Tewitfield and return, with a ninety minute stop at Bolton le Sands. A bus took the trippers back to their starting point. The above photo was taken on the Trust's first cruise in 1964 as the boat emerged from Deep Cutting to the South of Lancaster. The Trust also ran cruises to protest about the closing of the Upper Reaches to construct the M6 motorway. The photograph above left shows John Gavan of the Trust stood up at the back. Dan and Mary Ashcroft are at the tiller.

When commercial trade finished in 1947, and the last of the boats were dismantled and broken up only pleasure boats were seen on the canal. This one is in the former basin with Maudland Bank, Ashton. in the background.

A cruiser below is seen at Ashton, looking South, in the nineteen fifties with Tulketh Mill on the horizon.

An area known as the *'clay hills'*, about two miles from Preston basin, where clay was put onto the barges and taken along the canal to repair breaches. The houses in the background are in Stocks Road, Ashton and the site is now occupied by a building firm.

Dan Ashcroft, who had crewed many of the working boats, turned to running pleasure trips from the terminus at Aqueduct Street to the *'Jolly Roger'* at Catforth and back. He acquired the *'Shelagh'* which he brought from the Leeds-Liverpool Canal, across the Ribble and up to Glasson. These trips were a prominent feature of the canal for about twenty five years.

Dan and Mary at Galgate on *'Shelagh'*

Dan and his wife Mary "A real *'team'*

The canal has always been popular for leisure purposes, as this picture of skaters at Highgate Settings, Kendal shows. Also a popular feature were the day school and Sunday school outings on the well-scrubbed canal boats. These trips were sometimes known as *scholar boating* by the bargees. This picture is of the Zion Chapel Sunday School outing to Sedgwick, around the turn of the century.

Some of the boats look dangerously overcrowded. A church with a large congregation would hire two boats and sometimes take a piano on board. This postcard *"Lancaster Canal at Cottam Hall 1909"* shows around 200 people on the boat, as it approaches Bridge No. 16 at Cottam Hall, heading for Catforth.

The picture on the right is an outing of the Fylde Road Primitive Methodist Church in Preston taken about 1914 on one of the Baines Brothers boats, complete with gramophone. Lawrence Baines is on the left wearing his trademark bowler hat with his wife Mary on the right. The ladies on the front are thought to be members of the Ashcroft family. If one looks closely at the picture above, there is a man in a bowler hat stood up facing the bank, which could be Lawrence Baines.

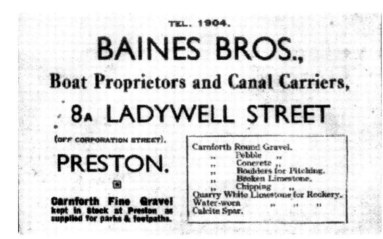

TEL. 1904.

BAINES BROS.,

Boat Proprietors and Canal Carriers,

8A LADYWELL STREET

(OFF CORPORATION STREET).

PRESTON.

Carnforth Fine Gravel
kept in stock at Preston as
supplied for parks & footpaths.

Carnforth Round Gravel.
 ,, Pebble ,,
 ,, Concrete ,,
 ,, Boulders for Pitching.
 ,, Broken Limestone.
 ,, Chipping ,,
Quarry White Limestone for Rockery.
Water-worn ,, ,, ,,
Calcite Spar.

Baines Brothers, Lawrence, James and John were the main carriers on the canal. When 'Wigan Coal & Iron' went out of business in 1928, the Baines' took over their fleet as well as the vessels of smaller companies such as Hampton's of Preston. When Baines Brothers ceased trading in 1944 they sold their boats to the bargees for £30 each.

Lawrence Baines' wife, Mary, ran a grocer's shop at No. 57 Marsh Lane, Preston, which is still there at the corner of Ladywell Street. The boat office had been formerly a public house called the 'Jolly Tars'.

The family, renowned for their 'good works', were stalwart members of the Fylde Road Primitive Methodist Church and supporters of the temperance movement in Preston. The ladies of the family used to bake cakes for the canal families and sometimes acted as midwives before the days of midwifery on the National Health Service. Lawrence Baines is stood at the rear of the boat in the bowler hat with his wife Mary in front of him, and members of the Ashcroft family.

Lawrence and Mary Baines and family c 1900. and right with two of their daughters and visiting Canadian soldiers at 57 Marsh Lane, during the First World War.

'May' No. 35' about 1910 with a cargo of stone near Garstang with the Baines family posing for the picture. Jack Baines, one of the Baines brothers, his daughter Elizabeth by his first wife Ellen, Janie his second wife and baby Tom. The *'Journal of Canal Inspections 1929-1938'* lists a total of seventeen boats in their ownership, having bought out the other traders on the canal.

Dan Ashcroft senior at Cottam Hall Bridge (No. 17) around 1900 on *'Redwing'* The patterns on the bow indicate that the vessel was owned by Thompson's of Lancaster. The Ashcrofts were one of the oldest families on the canal, going back at least five generations

Dan is pictured below on *'Kenneth'No. 41'* with his wife Alice, whose family, the Goodiers, were also connected with the canal.

By 1942 trade on this canal was dwindling but Dan, anxious that commercial trade should continue, formed his own company *'Ashcroft Carriers Ltd.'* along with his three sons, Dan, Joe and Jack to run the boats they had bought from Baines Brothers.

'Joseph No. 42' owned by one of the Baines Brothers, James, who as well as helping running the firm with Lawrence and Jack, was in the Preston Borough Police Force.

Joe and Dan, pictured here, were two of the sons of Dan Ashcroft senior and Alice (nee Goodier) and it was Joe who carried the last load to Storey's Mill in Lancaster in 1947. Storey's were the last firm to run on coal but after the bad winter that year when the canal was frozen and deliveries by boat were impossible for several weeks, they switched to oil, thus ending a long tradition heralding the end of commercial carrying on this canal.

Dan, who was born on *'Prince of Wales No. 3'* in 1908 married Mary Jane Robinson in 1931, thereby uniting two of the largest canal families. Mary Jane was born in 1914 and brought up with her parents, Thomas and Janet, brothers and sisters on Wigan Coal & Iron Company's boat *'Farewell No. 47'*. Dan and Mary Jane started their married life on *'May'* and worked both the Lancaster and the Leeds-Liverpool canals. Here we see Mary Jane in the stables at the rear of the former *'Boatman's Arms'* in Marsh Lane. Preston. Dan died in 1980 and Mary Jane in 2002.

Thomas and Fleetwood Ashcroft on
'Redwing' outside Lancaster in the
nineteen thirties. Thomas was the
uncle of Dan Ashcroft and worked
the canal with his wife Fleetwood
and young daughter May who took
these photographs with her 'Brownie'
camera.

Fleetwood at the
tiller. This Christian
name was given to
both males and
females.

Fleetwood was also from a canal family, the
Hardman's; her Christian name appears quite
often in the canal community. May (above) used
to regularly take the horses to the blacksmith for
shoeing, which cost about twelve shillings in the
1930s. She left the canal in 1939 for factory work
and died in 2004.

Wigan Coal & Iron's boat *'Express'* in 1929. Thomas Robinson is standing against the chimney which is made in two sections to enable them to be removed easily when entering low bridges. The little lad is his five year old grandson Joseph, who provided this photograph and many others from his family album. The lady peering through the hatch is Joe's mother Agnes and the picture was taken by Joe's father, Joseph Robinson senior.

Thomas was the grandfather of Mary Jane Ashcroft from the Robinson family. The Robinsons crewed many other boats such as *'Ann'* and *'Farewell'*, working mostly for Wigan Coal & Iron Company.

Father and son, Joe Robinson junior and senior

Three generations - Thomas Robinson and Joe senior and junior

Joseph Robinson junior on the *'forecastle'*

Two people at work on the canal wharf. An unknown boatman with the tools of his trade, bucket for the horse, and a short rope, possibly also for the horse. The photograph was taken about 1927 by Samuel Thompson on the wharf at Lancaster. The boatwoman is Alice (nee Hardman) wife of Richard Ashcroft. Her apron looks clean, so possibly taken at the start of the working day.

Thomas Ashcroft (right) with a very fine looking horse. Horses were mostly bought from dealers in Lancaster and all the Ashcroft men were known as *good horsemen*.

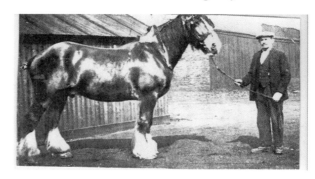

William Bewes with his wife Isabel and daughter Hilda, who provided this picture. He was a bank ranger from 1923 to 1954 and lived in Belmont Cottage, Hest Bank which is seen below. The boatmen used to moor at the cottage overnight to rest the horses and listen to William and Isabel's gramophone.

Belmont Cottage, long since demolished, had stables at one end, a large wash-house in the centre and living accommodation at the other end. There was no running water or electricity so they used paraffin lamps and water from a well behind the cottage.

An angler fishing by the canal at Highgate Settings, Kendal, now replaced by the A65 road to Burton.

These two photographs were taken in the 1930s at the scene of a serious breach of the canal bank at Cottam, near Preston. It is easy to tell who is in charge; the man in the bowler hat is giving instructions to the three workmen.

Boats lying idle at the basin at Maudland Bank during the 1921 coal strike. Tom Robinson (Mary's father) is the man in the braces. It was reported in the *'Lancashire Daily Post'* that *"many people have helped out their meagre supplies by 'fishing' for coal in the canal."*

Two views of Swillbrook Bridge (32). One is of the canal iced up in 1954, the other in Summer, showing it as a popular mooring spot. The main buildings are former stables, now dwelling houses and the area is commonly known as *'Jolly Roger'* named after the adjoining boatyard. In the days of the trip boat *'Shelagh'* the Jolly Roger was a café where the trippers used to partake of refreshment.

Another picture of the canal frozen up in 1963 at Ashton. The bank ranger who was responsible for the stretch of canal from Preston to Cadley lived in the house on the right of the picture, which is still there today.

Garstang Basin - The building on the left is the *'Tithebarn'* which predates the canal by about a hundred years. On the right is the Masonic Hall, demolished in 2007 to make way for a housing development and a new Masonic Hall. The *'Tithebarn'* is now a public house and restaurant, *'Th'owd Tithebarn'*, and the former wharf a popular mooring place.

'Tipsy Duck' moored at Th'owd Tithebarn

Carnforth Marina -- Carnforth grew from a small village with the coming of the canal and then the railway.

The Glasson branch was opened in 1826 and the canal junction is marked by the lock-keeper's cottage and a turnover bridge. There are six locks carrying the canal down to the sea, with another one down to Glasson Dock. The first lock-keeper was a James Bryce, who had formerly worked on the canal at Borwick. Unfortunately he drowned in the dock in 1835.

This terrible storm was photographed at the basin in 1928, with Pye's warehouse in the background. All these photographs of Glasson were taken by Fred Lamb, who made a unique photographic record of life in Glasson in the in the 1930s and 1940s.

Brant Breck Bridge (No. 91), entering Burrow Heights Cutting, more familiarly known as *'Deep Cutting'*. This was built through glacial deposits in order to avoid a long detour. The cutting is up to 10 metres deep and over 2 km. long. At the northern end of Deep Cutting is a view of Lancaster Castle. This was known to bargees as *Hangman's Corner'* as condemned prisoners were said to have exercised here.

'Redwing' in the ownership of Samuel Thompson & Co. of Lancaster outside Aldcliffe boathouse. The people seem to be dressed in their *'Sunday best'* for a trip out.

Canals were much favoured by photographers who were engaged in the publishing of picture postcards when they were much used as a means of communication in the first half of the twentieth century.

This is the much photographed Carr Lane Bridge (No 93) more commonly known as *'Broken Back Bridge'*.

Postcard entitled 'On *the Canal, Lea'*.
This picture is Cottam Mill (Bridge No. 16) looking South towards Preston. with Moon's Farm on the right.

The view left is not far from the appropriately named *'Packet Boat Inn'* at Bolton-le-Sands where the canal and the A6 road, a one-time turnpike, run close by each other, with the M6 motorway and the West Coast main railway line close by.

The postcard is entitled *'Slyne Bridge, Torrisholme'* but is known as *'Belmont Bridge'* (No. 114). The steps now have a handrail and the horizontal box and pipe are still there across the arch.

The Bolton le Sands area, because of its beautiful scenery, was much favoured for postcards of the Lancaster Canal. This one is undated and shows a lady, with a white apron, standing outside a cottage.

Mr. Vickers, *'dealer in hay and straw'* had his brick and coal yard in Canal Head North, Kendal. The dress of the man in the straw hat indicates that this photograph was taken in about 1900. The building is no longer there.

The *'Corporation Arms'* was next door to Waterhouse's grocers and general store in Penny Street, Lancaster. Men from the canal barges delivering coal to the area used to buy bread and cheese from the shop then take it into the pub, eat it for breakfast and wash the whole lot down with a glass of ale. It is unlikely that they would pay for the stabling facilities in a town centre pub (see the *'Good Stabling'* sign) when there were stables at the nearby wharf. The photograph dates from the latter half of the 19th century.

A *'bird's eye'* view of the Lune Aqueduct which was opened in 1797 at a cost of £48,000, taking five years to build. Designed by John Rennie and built of local stone, it measures 51 feet above the river and is 664 feet long. It is considered to be one of the most beautiful aqueducts in the country.

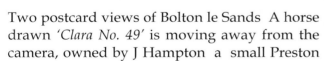

Two postcard views of Bolton le Sands A horse drawn *'Clara No. 49'* is moving away from the camera, owned by J Hampton a small Preston based canal carrier, who used to take the street sweepings out of Preston by boat along the canal for farmers to use as manure.   Two of their boats were called *'Harold No. 32'* and *'Venture No. 26'*.

The canal as seen from Parkside Bridge, Kendal formerly known as *'Gas Works Bridge'*. The end of the wharf projecting into the canal is shown on Hoggarths Map of 1853. Little of the original gas works remain apart from some workshops, now altered either side of the gate onto Parkside Road, formerly *'Gas House Lane'*.

A pleasant view of the canal going into Kendal, In 1942 a half mile section near Kendal Gas was closed. A 1955 Act of Parliament decreed that the canal be drained west of Stainton because of leakage and the last two miles to Kendal filled in.

On the Canal, Kendal.

This picture is entitled *"Around the Northern Reaches"* which refer to the isolated and un-navigable sections of the canal north of Tewitfield. The canal is still in water for a further eight miles to Stainton and can take small craft. The line of the canal to Kendal can still be followed on foot. Joe Robinson says the boatmen used to fill their water tanks up on the boat from the fresh unpolluted water here, which comes from the reservoir at Killington, the main feeder into the canal.

The old wharf that once served the village of Burton in Kendal pictured at Bridge No.144. c 1905. There is a pile of stones on the wharf and two boats are tied up, one of which is Baines Brothers *'May No., 35'*.

The old Tram Bridge in the 1860s taken from the south bank of the river looking up the Avenham incline, in a rather rickety state. The last coal wagon had used the bridge in 1862 and was now used only by pedestrians. This horse drawn tramway was only ever intended to be temporary. The original plan was for the southern section of the Lancaster Canal to start at Westhoughton, running on one level for 15 miles, and on to Chorley through Clayton Green. Thirty two locks would be built descending 222 feet to an embankment across the valley at Walton, crossing the River Ribble into Preston via an aqueduct over three arches, each of 116 feet span. It would then go on to Kendal via a second aqueduct crossing the Lune. This ambitious plan proved too expensive and never materialised.

In 1963 a new bridge was constructed to replace the one built a hundred and sixty years ago. The old bridge had been repaired by the Preston Corporation In 1936 torrential rainfall had almost washed the bridge away.

The *'Duke of York'* canal basin in Whittle le Woods, called after the pub. In 1816 when the Walton Summit arm was constructed to link the Leeds-Liverpool canal to the Lancaster Canal, millstones from the local quarry were despatched worldwide from this basin, which had a crane to load the millstones onto the boats, as well as wharves with coal yards, weighing machines and a smithy.
To get to the basin, boats coming from Chorley passed along the Lancaster canal and under the tunnels at Whittle. Stone from the quarries, coal and other goods were unloaded onto the wharf. This section of canal was drained in 1969 and the basin filled in and grassed over, after it had fallen into disuse.   Opposite the pub there is a monument, erected in 1985, consisting of four millstones, one of which was salvaged from the canal bed, erected to commemorate the history of the site.

Old barges at Walton Summit about 1900. The junction of the Walton Summit branch is at the bottom of the seven locks at Johnson's Hillock (seen below). These locks were built to connect the Leeds-Liverpool Canal to the Lancaster Canal at Whittle Springs basin. Part of this stretch is still in water but can only be followed a short way before it is obstructed by development.

Whittle Hill Tunnels were originally one single tunnel 259 yards long but after a collapse it opened up as two short tunnels with a 150 yard cutting between them. Aqueduct Bridge was built in 1760 to carry the Lancaster canal over the River Lostock leading to the tunnels at Whittle, which had fallen into decay but have now been cleared by volunteers.

Postcard of canal boat at Whittle-le-Woods

The old canal at Whittle and seen left is the basin just after draining in 1969.

Often referred to as the *'lost mile'* or *'Miley Green'* this is a view along the line of the filled-in and grassed over canal, which was in a cutting here, looking from Fylde Road and the University of Central Lancashire in the distance.

The present terminus at Ashton

Ashton Basin, after lying derelict for years. was restored in 1972 and boats can be hired from here.

This view is of Stocks Road Bridge (No. 11) at Ashton looking North. Bridges 1-10 have been filled in.

The Millennium Ribble Link completed in 2002 connects the Lancaster Canal into the Ribble Estuary so that boats can now cruise from the Link down the Ribble and Douglas rivers to the Rufford Branch of the Leeds and Liverpool Canal and then onto the rest of the inland waterways. There are nine locks including a sea lock and a three chambered staircase lock flight marks the entrance into the Link from the Lancaster. After the challenge of crossing the Link, the pace of life becomes immediately slower. *'Benjamin No. 48'* now sets off Southwards on the *'Lanky*, and Beetham's Farm seen on earlier photographs and which in the nineteen fifties sold sweets and ice-cream is on the right, now a private dwelling.

The fifteen foot statue at the start of the Sculpture Trail called *'Gauging the Ripple'* (the old name for the Ribble) and which represents the elements *earth' 'air' 'fire'* and *'water'*. Upper right is seen the first boat to enter the Millennium Link on the Commissioning Cruise held on 12 July 2002. The Link was opened officially on 20th September by the Rt. Hon. Margaret Beckett MP, Secretary of State for Environment, Food and Rural Affairs.

David and Alan Rigby and dog Charlie at the end of their journey on the new *'Benjamin No. 48'* in May 2005 having just entered the Lancaster Canal from the Ribble Link and the end of our journey along the *'Lanky'*.